G000112862

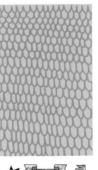

IRON ME ON

WELCOME TO THE WORLD OF IRON-ONS!

With these decal-based iron-on transfers, you will be able to create one-of-a-kind wearable art and gifts featuring the eye-catching art and alphabets of illustrator Mike Perry. Inside, you'll find twenty pages of patterns, images, and text that can be mixed and matched to create designs for T-shirts, tote-bags, pillow cases, hats, and any other fabric surface you can dream of.

Using iron-on decals is simple and fun. All you need is an iron, a steady hand, a fabric of your choice, and a flat, hard surface. But if you're new to iron-ons, or just need a refresher, there are few things you should know before you begin.

CHOOSING YOUR FABRIC

Iron-on transfers can be applied to most cotton-based fabric, but they tend to work best on smooth material (like a T-shirt or handkerchief). Avoid applying transfers to rough or textured materials (such as heavy canvas) as the bumps and ridges in the fabric will affect the quality of the transfer.

The designs in this book can be used in a variety of ways. There are stand-alone images that you can cut out and use as the centerpiece for a T-shirt, and there are some full-bleed patterns, like the bricks, from which you can cut out custom shapes to print whatever you want. Mix and match to create your own designs or borders, or you can write your name or a phrase by cutting out and arranging letters from the typeface pages. Be sure to plan your design ahead of time by mapping it out on the garment you plan to use. Remember the old maxim of "measure twice, cut once," when planning your design.

YOUR IRON

Once you've prepared your design, the next step is to apply it to your garment. Use a high-quality iron set to high heat or cotton. Make sure to turn the steam feature off and remove any water from the iron's reservoir. Before you begin to apply the transfers, the iron should be hot—heat and even pressure are the keys to a quality iron-on transfer.

YOUR WORKSPACE

Choose a smooth, hard surface as your workspace—such as a worktable or bench, a Formica countertop or piece of smooth plywood—don't use an ironing board, as it won't hold the necessary heat. Cover your workspace with an old sheet, pillowcase, or other smooth fabric. Make sure there are no wrinkles or ridges in your workspace.

TIME TO IRON-ON!

1. Iron your garment to make sure there are no wrinkles and lay it flat on your workspace. Arrange your design on your fabric decal-side down (remember that the images reverse in the transfer, so if you're using letters to spell out a word or phrase, make sure you've planned it out correctly).

2. Lay your iron down on the center of your transfer and apply light but even pressure. Move your iron over the transfer in slow circles from the outer edges towards the center of the transfer. The transfer should start right away as the glue from the decals begins to merge with the fabric. The entire process should take roughly 2 to 4 minutes, depending on the heat of your iron and the quality of the fabric.

With decal-based transfers, a little finesse goes a long way. Too much time under the iron can burn and crack the decal, too little will make it difficult to remove—it takes patience and practice, especially if you are working over a large area. Work in stages!

3. Once your transfer is complete, remove from heat and let the decal cool slightly. Slowly peel the decal backing away from the fabric.

4. Enjoy your creation!

IRON-ON TIPS AND TRICKS:
Unless you consider yourself an iron-on expert, do a few tests on spare garments before creating your iron-on masterpiece. Iron temperatures vary and different fabrics react differently to the heat transfer, so there will always be some trial and error that you will need to work through.

To easily apply the proper amount of pressure (30 to 50 pounds) try working on a surface lower than a conventional table top so that you can use your upper body to add weight to the iron without too much effort.

Be careful! Irons are hot and, at least during the process, your garment will be hot and the decal sheets will be hot. Always use caution—and remember that the transfer images can bleed through your garment (and on to your workspace) or burn if left under the heat too long.

WASHING AND CARE OF YOUR IRON-ON GARMENT:
With a little extra care, your iron-on transfer should weather the laundry cycle well. Turn your garment inside out and wash it on the gentle cycle in cold water using color safe detergent. Air dry or run through a dryer on low heat.

Mike Perry is a graphic designer and typographer in Brooklyn. He's the author of **Hand Job** and **Over & Over**. For more of Mike's work, including printed T-shirts, visit www.mikeperrystudio.com.

ISBN: 978-0-8118-7726-8
Manufactured in China
Design by Mike Perry
Typeset in Bryant and Trade Gothic

10 9 8 7 6 5 4 3 2 1

CHRONICLE BOOKS
680 SECOND STREET
SAN FRANCISCO, CA 94107
WWW.CHRONICLEBOOKS.COM